AMAZING
SCIENCE

Flakes and Flurries
A Book About Snow

by **Josepha Sherman**   illustrated by **Jeff Yesh**

Thanks to our advisers for their expertise, research, knowledge, and advice:

Mark W. Seeley, Ph.D., Professor of Meteorology and Climatology
Department of Soil, Water, and Climate
University of Minnesota, St. Paul

Mike Graf, M.A., Instructor of Child Development
Chico (California) State University

Susan Kesselring, M.A., Literacy Educator
Rosemount-Apple Valley-Eagan (Minnesota) School District

PICTURE WINDOW BOOKS
Minneapolis, Minnesota

Managing Editor: Bob Temple
Creative Director: Terri Foley
Editors: Sara E. Hoffmann, Michael Dahl
Editorial Adviser: Andrea Cascardi
Copy Editor: Laurie Kahn
Designer: Nathan Gassman
Page production: Picture Window Books
The illustrations in this book were rendered digitally.

Picture Window Books
5115 Excelsior Boulevard
Suite 232
Minneapolis, MN 55416
1-877-845-8392
www.picturewindowbooks.com

Printed in the United States of America.

Library of Congress Cataloging-in-Publication Data
Sherman, Josepha.
Flakes and flurries : a book about snow / by Josepha Sherman ;
illustrated by Jeff Yesh. v. cm. — (Amazing science)
Includes bibliographical references and index.
Contents: Snow and rain—Snow crystals make snowflakes—
Crystal shapes—Snowflakes have six sides—Listen to the snow—
Mountain snow—Blizzards and sleet.
ISBN 1-4048-0098-0
1. Snow—Juvenile literature. [1. Snow.]
I. Yesh, Jeff, 1971- ill. II. Title.
QC926.37 .S48 2003
551.57'84—dc21
                                        2003004704

Table of Contents

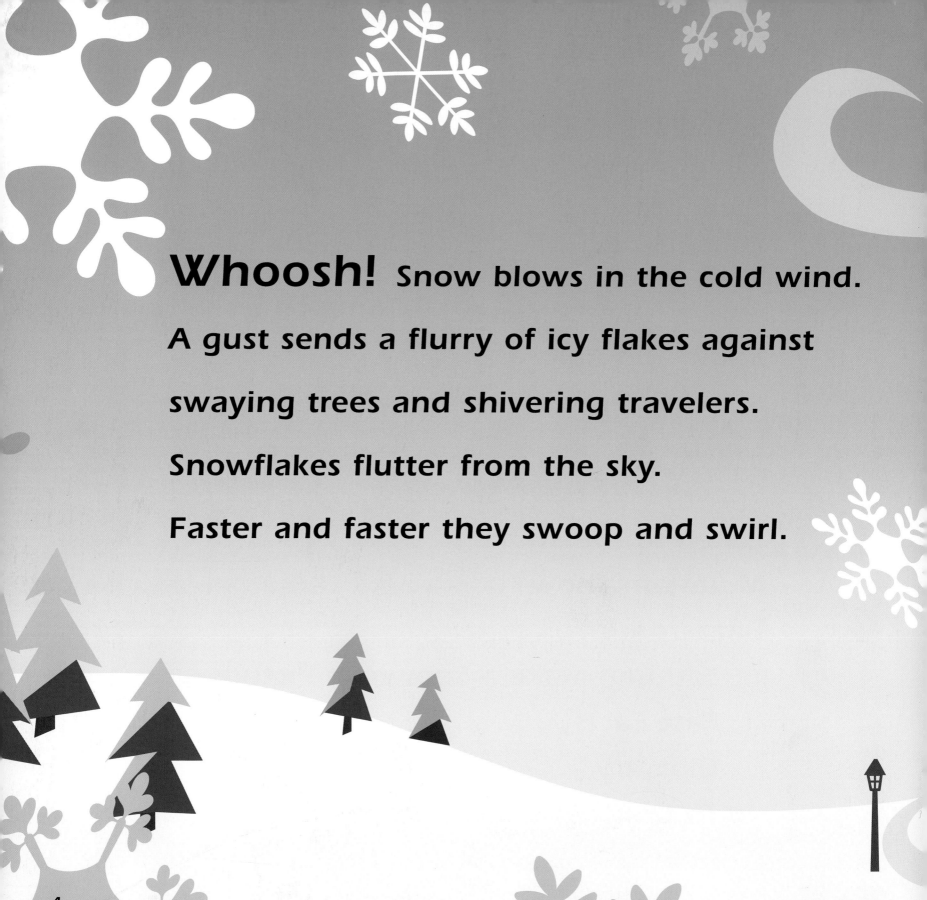

Whoosh! Snow blows in the cold wind.

A gust sends a flurry of icy flakes against

swaying trees and shivering travelers.

Snowflakes flutter from the sky.

Faster and faster they swoop and swirl.

4

Snow and Rain

Snow falls from clouds like rain.

Rain falls as water droplets.

Snow falls as icy crystals.

Snow falls mostly in winter,
when the air is cold.

Snow Crystals Make Snowflakes

A snow crystal is a tiny bit of ice. The ice is water that freezes around a speck of dust floating in the air. Several snow crystals join together to make a snowflake.

A snowflake is made of at least two crystals.
Some snowflakes are made of 100 crystals or more.

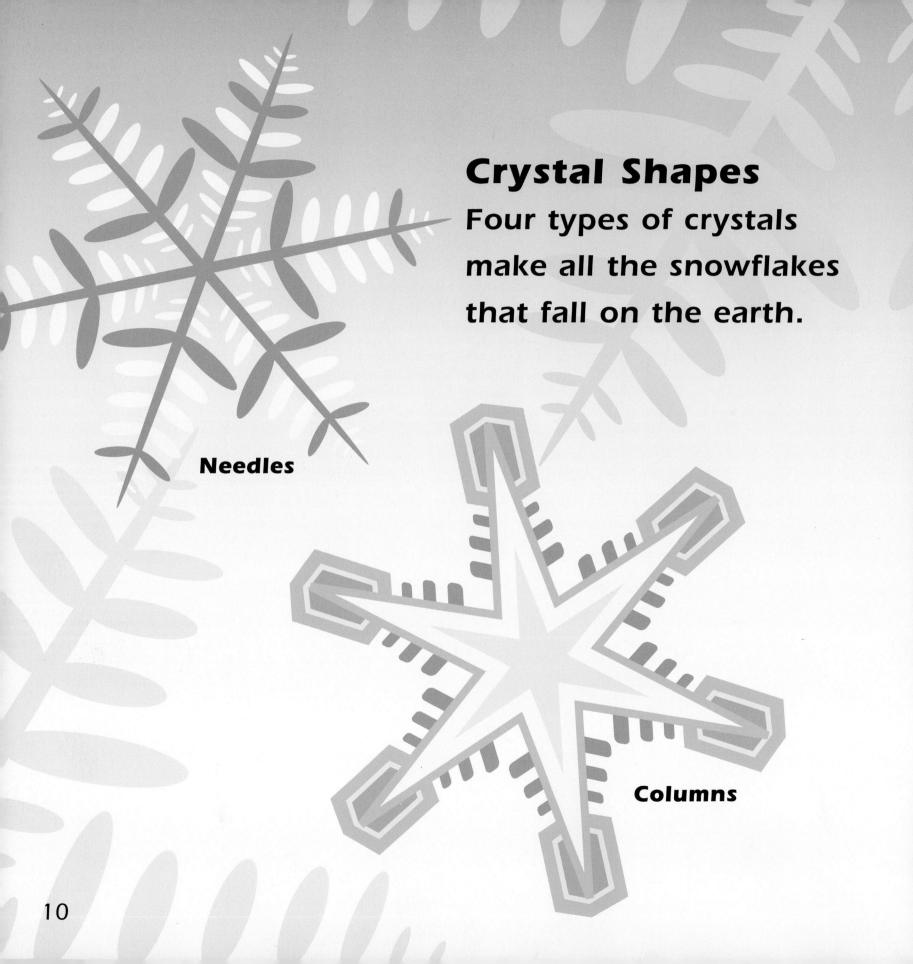

Crystal Shapes

Four types of crystals make all the snowflakes that fall on the earth.

Needles

Columns

10

The shape of a snowflake depends on the air temperature. If the temperature is very low, columns, thin plates, and sector plates appear on snowflakes.

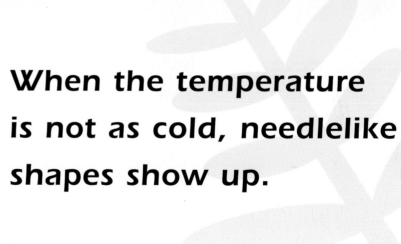

Sector Plates

Thin Plates

When the temperature is not as cold, needlelike shapes show up.

Snowflakes Have Six Sides

Catch a floating flake on your mitten or glove. See how every delicate flake has six sides? Even so, no two flakes look alike.

Listen to the Snow

Walk across the cold snow.

Hear it crunch and squeak beneath your boots?

Snow crystals have open spaces that hold air.
When you walk on the snow, you break
the crystals. The broken crystals snap,
and the air escapes in crunches and pops.

Mountain Snow

A lot of snow falls in the mountains.
That is because it is very cold there.
People in the mountains enjoy
winter sports such as skiing,
sledding, and snowboarding.

In the spring, when the sun gets higher
and stronger, melting snow trickles
into rivers and streams. Mountain snow
melts into water for crops and animals.

17

Blizzards

Blizzards are powerful and dangerous snowstorms. A blizzard can bring high winds, colder temperatures, and heavy snow. It can last for hours.

18

Blowing snow piles up on roads, slowing down travelers. Street signs and familiar sights are hidden behind a world of whirling white.

After a snowstorm, bundle up and run outside.
Cold air greets your face. Sunlight shines
on the fallen snow. Millions of dazzling crystals
reflect the light.

Build a snowman. Hurl a snowball.
Make snow angels on the ground.
Plow down a hill of powdery snow on your sled.
Nature's winter playground surrounds you.

You Can Make a Snowman Picture

What you need:

- a tablet of multicolored construction paper
- a pencil or pen
- cotton balls
- glue
- scissors
- crayons or markers

What you do:

1. Make sure you have an adult help you.

2. Choose a sheet of construction paper. This will be the background for your snowman picture. Pick a color that is light enough to draw on, such as white or pale blue.

3. Use the pencil or pen to draw an outline of a snowman on the construction paper. Be creative—your snowman could be made of two snowballs, three snowballs, or more.

4. Build your snowman by using the cotton balls to fill in the outline you've drawn. Glue the cotton balls in place.

5. Cut out different colored scraps of construction paper to give your snowman eyes, a nose, a mouth, a hat, and any other decorations you'd like. Glue the decorations to your snowman.

6. Draw a background for your snowman. This background will be your snowman's home. Does he live at the North Pole? In your backyard?

Fast Facts

- Buffalo, New York, is one of the snowiest cities in the United States. In December 2001, a blizzard dumped almost seven feet (two meters) of snow on the city in one week. Schools were closed, cars were buried, and no one could fly in or out of the Buffalo airport.

- Almost every place in the United States has had snowfall at one time or another. Even southern Florida has seen snow flurries.

- Snow can be a lot of fun, but too much snow can be dangerous. People who climb mountains have to watch out for avalanches. An avalanche is when a very large amount of snow falls down the side of a mountain. In a big avalanche, there is enough snow to fill 20 football fields with piles 10 feet (3 meters) deep.

- In Bratsk, Siberia, someone once found a snowflake as big as a sheet of notebook paper!

Glossary

blizzard—a powerful snowstorm with heavy winds, blowing snow, and falling temperatures

flurry—a brief shower of blowing snow

gust—a short rush of wind

reflect—to throw back light

snow crystal—a tiny bit of ice that has frozen in a pattern around a speck of dust

To Learn More

At the Library

Branley, Franklyn M. *Snow Is Falling.* New York: HarperCollins Publishers, 2000.

Owen, Andy. *Snow.* Des Plaines, Ill.: Heinemann Library, 1999.

Schaefer, Lola M. *A Snowy Day.* Mankato, Minn.: Pebble Books, 2000.

On the Web

For Kids Only: Earth Science Enterprise
http://kids.earth.nasa.gov
For information on NASA and how its scientists study air, water, and land

The National Severe Storms Laboratory's Weather Room
http://www.nssl.noaa.gov/edu
For fun, basic information on weather for kids, parents, and teachers

Fact Hound
Fact Hound offers a safe, fun way to find Web sites related to this book. All of the sites on Fact Hound have been researched by our staff.
http://www.facthound.com

1. Visit the Fact Hound home page.

2. Enter a search word related to this book, or type in this special code: 1404800980.

3. Click on the FETCH IT button.

Your trusty Fact Hound will fetch the best sites for you!

Index